Poetry and More

From a NICU Nurse

By

Leilani K. Ruland, RN

Copyright ©2018 Leilani Ruland

All rights reserved

Dedicated to my grandchildren

Megan, Mickey, Kacey, Liam, Ethan, Elliot, and Julian

Journey on

"After the first death there is no other."

— Dylan Thomas, 1914 – 1953

A Refusal to Mourn the Death, by Fire, of a Child in London

Author's Note and Acknowledgements

I want to thank the nurses, doctors, and healthcare professionals I had the privilege to work with during my nursing career. It was a blessing to care for the tiny human beings who passed briefly through my hands. I will forever be grateful to their families for sharing their lives with me.

I also want to thank my husband, Frederick, for his assistance and support in proving the power of love, as we celebrate fifty-three years of life together.

Note that no actual names have been used in these works.

Contents:

Keeping Noah Here
In Defense of Two Tower North 1984
Endings
April Son
The Boy Who Mowed My Yard
Ballad of Gloria
To Beltiffinase on Her Sixth Week Birthday
For Don – RT 1980
From the Diary of a Nurse (for a boy dying of AIDS – age nineteen)
Eulogy for Howie – Age Four Months
Jeremy
Mother Loss 1994
No Time to Cry
The Color of David – Aged eleven
Unknown SYNDROME
Vigil (for Jeffrey)
For Adam

Keeping Noah here

Two pounds, your
28-week arrival has stunned me.
you lie in the artificial womb
tied to machines that chirp like crickets.
I am only armed with prayers and
hopes and dreams
that tumble around in my head.
But, I am your strong voice.

On this warm October evening
my comfort comes in bits,
holding a tiny hand as you
suck wildly, briefly on
the spaghetti-thin tube
that slides into a belly
waiting to welcome my milk.

I touch your perfect body,
my breasts aching for your eyes to
open,
searching for something of me.
Will the face of your father surface?

I count your heartbeats
dancing double-time with mine.
I cry with every needle stick
that draws your blood.

They shave your head to find a vein,
I keep the bit of dark hair.
your day ends with a step backward.

"Be strong," they tell me, "He knows
you are here."
What do I know about courage?

Each night I lie awake beside a cradle,
my hand where your head should be.

The phone rings, calling me back to
your side.
I stand trembling
while you are dragged through yet
another crisis.

I beg you, stay another day for me.

In Defense of Two Tower North
1984

On the tower
where miracles sometimes happen
I can show you enough pain
to break your heart

days are long here
longer than twenty-four hours
ask any parent
to tell you about futures
they live in the present,
'one day at a time,' sweet Jesus.

breath sounds are loud in this room
the alarms frightening
sudden death
brings us all to our knees

spend some time here
touch a baby
smaller than your own hand
see his heart beat
place him in his mother's arms
watch her hold him close
    under blazing lights
that cook her, keeping him warm

see the bone-weary interns
dressed in wrinkled blue, sweating,
somehow getting a second burst of energy
after thirty-six hours on their feet
when the blood gas improves
smiling their sense of wonder
here
standing on holy ground

watch the nurses
counting heartbeats
humming softly
rocking
praying
crying
hoping

it's the little things that count
on the tower

Endings

a late child is a blessing, mother said,
it makes you young again.
How much he wanted a girl. Fancy
dresses and patent shoes stand out
in a world full of sneakers and jeans.
She pounded on that old piano
for hours, I prayed for silence.
Now, I have it. All those nights I
dragged myself out of bed and found
him there. Even in that wasted
face her eyes were birthday blue.
I'll pack up all those pastels, funny
how she liked to dress in red. I'll have
my sewing room again. The boys
won't have to share. The pain ripples
through my head like a tooth gone bad.
On this empty, leafless January night,
I sit listening,
in the silence of her room,
her name stuck in my throat.

April Son

Today your brother asked about you
wondering like children do about death
you are ten long years gone
dead in my womb at five months

when they finally separated us
in that sterile, cold, white-walled room
I was in a sleep – the artificial sleep
invented for doctors – they put me under
and took you away

I never held you, touched you, named you
your daddy drove one hundred miles
to bury one small white box
beside a grandfather he never knew

if I had it to do over
I would hold you long enough to
memorize your features
long enough to say goodbye

now, all I can do
is write this poem
giving your brother
something to remember you by

1985

The Boy Who Mowed My Yard
(née a two-pound preemie)

I knew him when he was a boy,
he mowed my yard one summer.
I gave him twenty-five cents
and all the cookies he could eat.

His family lived across the alley
over Thompson's Drugstore
seven children
slept in blankets on the floors
of three windowless rooms.

He could eat a pound of Pecan Sandies
in one sitting.
his brown eyes burned with dreams as
he talked of engineering a giant
locomotive.
I remember his skinny elbows,
the color of oyster shells,
peeking through the jean jacket
with cigarette burns.
He kept his money
(I found it last summer)
under the stairwell that led
into my basement. He was gone then,
lost,
out of my reach.

His mother never
dressed him warm enough
and he was always alone.
Sometimes he paused on my back steps
to play with my arthritic cat who loved him.
She would come off the porch-swing
limping
on stiff legs to cuddle on his lap.
He wept when she died
helped me bury her
under the crooked maple.
He dragged a stone
halfway across town
to mark her grave.

His father wandered off
making him head of the household
at thirteen.

Paper says he is twenty-five now
and that an old night watchman is
dead.

I never saw him play.

Ballad of Gloria

    'I'm sorry', the doctor said.
    'She's not coming out of this coma.'

Oh, Lord, we do not know the reason why
our Gloria's asleep,
but she is loved and warm and dry,
and kept so by her mother's gentle hands.

When she was born that windy April day,
they placed her in our open arms,
all wrapped in fuzzy pink,
she briefly opened eyes that caught blue light.

    Forgive us Lord if now and then we weep,
        while rocking our sweet Gloria, asleep.

This child who shares our name is three months old,
the unknown virus stopped her fragile hold on life, now stealing her away.

Each night I sit beside her maple crib,
the closet filled with clothes still tagged and new.
Her toys sit silently . . . she does not care.

A week ago she looked into my face then smiled and drifted off
into her secret place.
Her hair is soft and silky on my hands.

        Forgive us Lord if now and then we weep,
        while rocking our sweet Gloria, asleep.

To Beltiffinase on Her Sixth Week Birthday

I call your name, child, the newness in the sound rolls off my tongue like a foreign language. Bel……tiff…..in…ase. Your mother made it up, insisted that we not give you a nickname. Still, I sing for you, for your sweet breath against my hand, like the kiss of a moth, hallelujah, you are at last breathing on your own. One pound, two ounces, you lie in your heated incubator, misted oxygen blowing into your face while your chest moves in a perfect rhythm that matches my own heartbeat.

I shall chart in my nurse's notes that your color is pink, at least the nail beds under the ebony skin that is now a shade darker than your mother's.

It was exactly six weeks ago that I got the call.

"We're bringing one in to die," the medic in a squad told me. You were born at home, in the middle of the night to a fifteen-year-old who had told nobody about her pregnancy. You were a one pound quivering blue bit of humanity that arrived to us by a squad. You were so cold that your body temperature didn't register on the thermometer. We calculate twenty-four week gestation as we observe you. Your eyelids are still fused like a newborn kitten. The decision was made to keep you warm and dry but, no other medical intervention would be attempted. You were at the cut-off age for life. Best to do nothing.

For six hours you continued to gasp as your immature lungs struggled for each breath.

You did not die. The doctors began to argue among themselves. What to do? In anguish, but without hope, they decide to put you on the respirator in an attempt to ease your struggle to breathe. How hard the decisions that are made by the hour. How easily we might have given up.

"We have to at least try," the resident said. "She is holding on, doing her part."

It is my job to thread a needle as thin as a pencil lead into a leg vein and begin the necessary fluids.

The doctor did his part as he placed the line through your umbilical cord where we could monitor your blood gases. Something we could monitor before making other decisions.

We were all caught up now in the game of your life.

Now it was up to you.

When I returned the next evening, I was stunned to find you still here. The report was worrisome. Your gases were stable, but your chest X-rays were troublesome.

I understood something I hadn't admitted to myself last night – I wanted you to live.

No miracles yet, but you were still here. You were a pathetic sight, covered in bruises that were already turning into various shades of purple and blue.

Your mother had named you, still a child herself, somewhere else in this hospital fighting an infection. Your name was longer than your body. Something we could joke about. Something we might share with each other in this frightening place.

Jokes or not, you made it through your first week. On your eighth day of life disaster struck. Your heart stopped four times. We started you on three emergency drugs, one to keep your heart rate up, one to keep your blood pressure stable, and one for pain.

In an eight-hour period you blew three tiny holes in your lungs, and we caught them on X-ray. Each time the intern sutured a chest tube in place he swore it would be the last one.

You defied us all. You would go for hours looking as if your death was eminent, then you'd rally – were you testing us?

The night your grandmother brought your mother into the room they could not look at you without weeping.

"She looks like a little plucked chicken," your mother said. She would not touch you. Sadly, I watched them detach from you.

"We won't be back," your grandmother said. "She's not going to make it. I can't take any more of this."

Although my heart was heavy when I looked at you – tortured with the treatments – I knew that we had never tried to force life into you. It was always there, hidden somehow, in your tiny self.

On your tenth day of life you opened your eyes!

You continued to survive all the many crises that every premature infant fights.

Slowly the days passed. Some were good. Some were bad.

Every nurse in that unit had spent a shift with you. We all knew how hard you struggled, but refused to die.

There was something unique about you. There was nobody calling to check on you. No visitors. You belonged to us and every doctor assigned to our unit had spent some time caring for you.

The more you demanded of us the more we had to give.

Today, you showed us that you could breathe on your own. Best of all, on your sixth week birthday, you reminded us that nothing is black or white. Doctors and nurses don't know everything. We still grope, often blindly, for the right thing to do. We, too, suffer with our decisions.

I pause at your warming bed, I hold your hand, smaller than my thumbnail. "Happy birthday, Beltiffinase." Your tiny fingers wrap instinctively around my own.

Incredible. You are still here.

For Don – RT 1980

figures dancing in his brain
CO_2
PO_2
pH
sending signals to his fingers
that control the buttons
on the $20,000 machine
monitoring the baby
    the tiny pair of immature lungs
    keep on moving
    in and out
    racing desperately
    against the disease

this man
my comrade
feeds me all his knowledge
in the sterile white room of noises

333
call this number
when in danger
he'll come running
up and down back stairs
    you can bag-breathe forever
      so the doctor says
Don knows better
so do I
death hangs heavy in the air
still, we try

**From the Diary of a Nurse
(for a boy dying of AIDS – age nineteen)**

He lives in isolation, gowned, gloved,
and masked, I enter his room.
this boy guitarist, his music stopped,
skin spotted like red jewels
on white sand.

his mother, a friend, has asked
me to visit.
He knows.

"I'm dead already to my family."
He chokes with coughing, lungs greedy
for air. Bones shine through a luminous face,
the congested eyes full of ghosts.
He can't eat. I touch a wrist, feel
the pulse racing towards infinity.

"Hey Joe," I say, "Do you remember
me rocking you as a baby? Is there
pain?"

"The pain of knowledge we don't
know."
He weeps, I sense his spirit
withdrawing,
blood sprays his cracked lips.

we will come to learn about this disease
but not here, not today.

Later, off duty, I sit with him,
the dark piling around us, as his hard
whispered breaths begin slowing.
I remove my rubber gloves, letting
my warm flesh tell him goodbye.

Eulogy for Howie – Age Four Months

On a balmy January evening
he left us,
traveling faster than light,
he came up on the other side of the
sun,
flew to the edge of the universe
and burst
into heaven
like a yellow butterfly
leaving his pain behind.

In our hospital room, full of sick babies,
there is no time for weeping,
so we journey on.

Heaven was ready,
all the shimmering angels,
mouths full of poetry,
welcomed him,
kissing the pale baby cheeks
into roses.

He lifts up his hands,
as the splendor
of a breeze purring against his throat
wraps around him giving comfort.
The hole, no longer needed
for breathing, closes, and he smiles.

His laughter bubbles out like
never ending wind chimes.
He sees hundreds of bluebirds
as the angels fly around him,
fitting miniature wings
onto his rounded shoulders.

They feed him
tart raspberry ice cream,
letting it drip from his mouth.
It touches the ground and tulips
spring into life tickling his baby feet
and the needle marks disappear like
magic.

Do not weep for him now,
he sits among the angels,
listen,
you can hear him singing,
he is so full of life,
he makes Jesus laugh.

Jeremy

The last warm feelings of safety disappeared, along with the comfort from the pounding of his mother's heart. Strong, gloved hands were holding him.

Jeremy was born.

He opened his eyes for a brief moment, but the lights were dazzling, and so he closed them again. The voices were loud and buzzing in his ears.

"Come on, little fellow, and breathe!" the doctor demanded. Someone rubbed his back and slapped the bottom of his feet.

Jeremy was born at 34 weeks. He had Hyaline membrane disease, a serious respiratory disorder when his *lungs weren't ready. His first breath was agony. Several quick breaths followed, and then he rested. He was cold, and his skin was blue. A mist of oxygen was blowing into his face.*

"Not good enough. We'll have to help him breathe," the doctor told his father. A tube was forced down his throat and into his lungs, and suddenly Jeremy found relief. He no longer had to breathe for himself. Now he could rest. Someone jabbed a needle into his arm and tied it down. He was too tired to care. He went to sleep.

Jeremy didn't hear them bring his mother to his side. He never felt her trembling hands stroke his small forehead or take his tiny hand into her own. He didn't see the tears in her eyes or the pain etched into the face of his father. He knew nothing of the long ambulance ride to a special unit for sick newborns in Columbus, Ohio.

He awakened briefly several hours later. There were many new noises here. Someone said, "He's getting worse. We'll have to increase his oxygen. The disease won't peak for two more days. We'll have to wait and see."

He could hear the fast pace of his own heartbeat on the monitor over his head. The gentle swishing of the respirator lulled him back into sleep.

Now it was morning, and he was 24 hours old. Still the disease raged. He fought the respirator. Gentle hands tried to soothe his restlessness, and a voice whispered.

"Come on, little fellow, and rest."

"Good boy, Jeremy, let the machine do the breathing."

"Your daddy's here, old man."

He didn't try to open his eyes again. He knew the bright lights would still be there.

Another day passed and then another and they were much the same. Still, he struggled. He was so tired. It was impossible now to fight the respirator. He let it breathe for him. He couldn't even cry. The tube prevented this.

The next time he awakened very quietly. He lay still and listened. He was 74 hours old.

"Hey!" Someone yelled excitedly. "The blood gases are good! I think he's

better. Let's try coming down on his oxygen."

He could breathe a little on his own. He didn't feel as tired. Everyone seemed so excited. He didn't know his father was there until he felt the tears falling onto his arm.

"Ah now, Jeremy," the doctor said. "It's time to pull the tube and see if you can do it all by yourself."

And so the tube was pulled, and he was ready. He tried a breath or two. It didn't seem so hard. The pain was gone, and so he tried another, and another. Soon they fell into a regular pattern. His heart rate speeded up, but remained steady. The cool mist was once again blowing into his face. This time it brought relief. He was warm. His body was pink. He found his fingers. Sucking wildly, he felt his first pangs of hunger. He drifted in and out away from all the noises, the happy voices.

His father's laughter brought him fully awake. For the first time he knew he was safe.

Someone gently picked him up and wrapped him in a blanket. Misty mask and all, he was placed in his mother's arms. The warmth of her body spread rapidly through him.

"Hi Jeremy," her soft voice whispered.

He opened his eyes. The bright lights were gone.

Everyone cheered!

Jeremy went back to sleep.

Mother Loss
1994

the pain in my gut
stops my breathing
he is out
twenty-four week birthday
one pound
black hair, naked
his cold little belly
like satin on my hand

I couldn't keep him warm

every finger and toe,
even his rosebud mouth,
perfect

no sweet breaths
on my cheek to treasure

he never opened his eyes.

unfolded flower
he left the world
taking back into infinity
his dreams along with
a piece torn from my heart
a wound that won't scar

what does it matter
that my breasts ache

who will I live for now?

No Time To Cry

It is 1987

I am on duty in the neonatal nursery.

It is December, a cold, blustery, freezing rain.

I am up for the next admission. Life Flight will bring him to me.

I get all the details of his premature birth. In the early darkness, on a rain-slicked highway 100 miles north of Columbus, a tractor trailer has skidded and rammed a small car carrying a young woman swollen with pregnancy. The baby is born in that tangled wreckage. His mother is lost to us. Less than 2 pounds, three months early, as the transport nurse tells me over the *telephone. They will have him here in 25 minutes.*

I hang up the phone and look around. Thirteen babies in this room where miracles sometimes happen. I can show you enough pain to break your heart. Days are long here. Breath sounds are loud, the alarms frightening, sudden death brings us all to our knees.

Spend some time here. Touch a baby — not much larger than your hand — dressed in doll clothes. Place him in his mother's arms. Watch her hold him under blazing lights that cook her, but keep him warm. Six nurses in this room, everyone busy, keeping tiny hearts beating. I shave a head to find a vein, the mother keeps that wisp of hair. She cries with every needle stick that draws his blood.

Meet Joshua, 4 months old now and tipping the scales at 4 pounds. He is ready to go home. We will celebrate with a cake baked by his grandmother.

I am called to Noah's warming bed. Three weeks old today and still dangerously ill, he has dragged through yet another crisis. His mother clings to my hand. Her comfort comes from minor things, holding a hand as small as the tip of her thumb. I leave his side, letting his mother keep her vigil.

Using the unit camera, I photograph Katy, she is 7 hours old. A small gold cross is taped to her bed. She is being held awkwardly by a first-time father. An oxygen mask covers the tiny mouth and nose. Nevertheless, Katy sucks on a small blue pacifier.

I telephone her mother, still in a hospital in Wheeling, WV. I tell her Katy is breathing better. When I mention that Katy is in her daddy's arms, she thanks me and begins to weep. I picture her in that lonely bed, her arms empty. I tell her I am sending her two pictures of Katy, something to hold onto until she's well enough to travel here.

I think about Benjamin who died today. He was 19 days old, 2 pounds, 3 ounces, yet already developing an amazing personality.

He fought the respirator, the warming bed, his heat shield, and when he peed all over the lab technician, everyone laughed. His mother held him for less than 60 minutes. His death will touch a grandfather 500 miles away, and across the ocean an uncle will weep.

I hear the thumping of Life Flight. My own heart races. Five minutes later he is wheeled into the nursery, a tiny boy buried in a sea of wires and plastic tubing. He is blue. His skin is transparent and bruised.

Scared voices bark out orders. A doctor pumps a chest as fragile as an eggshell. I gently squeeze the black bag forcing air into the immature lungs.

Oh baby don't die . . . my silent plea . . .

We work frantically as the minutes creep by. Nothing helps. We are all holding our breaths until a doctor stops the action. He turns off the machines. Someone has to do it.

I am left to care for him. I feel his warmth slipping away as he fades into infinity.

I wrap the perfectly formed body into a soft blue blanket and carry him into the treatment room.

My shift is almost over. His blood dries on my scrubs. I sit rocking him against my own heart.

Somewhere on a freeway, a father is speeding toward Columbus. He is coming here, to him.

The Color of David
Aged eleven

Migrating Monarch

  sprinkling butterfly kisses

    on the blue silk roses

      blanketing his grave.

Unknown SYNDROME

Lord, I can't explain him,
doctors don't know why
the small brown gold-flecked eyes
rarely close
constant energy
babbling sounds,
attempts to walk,
all documented in his baby book.
for posterity

His long afternoon naps
in his sibling's tooth-scarred crib,
netted for safety
freed me to join a host of
neighborhood mothers.

I drink warmed-over tea
steeped in soap operas
hear about
children
who absorb knowledge
like cereal soaking up milk.

I smile, accepting the comfort
of understanding friends
no answers here

I don't speak of
extra-armed chromosomes,
an under-developed heart
a life span of maybe seven years

at night
I sing him to sleep
sweet lullaby of him
holding him
like a small perfumed pillow
until he lets go of my hair
and drifts into blessed sleep

I stand at his blue-curtained window
weary from the never-ending day
I watch the perfect moon climb
over my misery
listening until I hear again
his wail on that day
he leaped from my womb

Vigil
(for Jeffrey)

I stand at his bedside, breathe with the respirator
the monitor matches the beating of two hearts
forgive me nurse, if I seem distant, make your
work more difficult. he is your patient, my son,
eight hours of his day belong to you.

twelve years I had him. you wait for a lunch break,
I wait for a miracle. your eyes are filled with hope,
his eyes are closed.

my unshed tears will fill this room

dear God, please make him whole again,
let him walk, run, fight with his brother, kiss his mother, hold my hand, call me daddy.

Please give him back to me
Jeffrey, my son

For Adam

Adam died today in my
NICU
He was nineteen days old.
At two pounds, three ounces,
You might picture a miniature old man,
with hair all over his body,
but not an ounce of fat.

Born three months early,
he was in his mother's arms
when he left us. His father
rubbed the tiny head, then wiped his
nose on his shirt like a wayward child.

Eyes cloud over as we wonder why
the skill of all our doctors and
highly trained nurses could not save
him.

This small poem is written in his memory.
I imagine all the years ahead without Adam.
Like a pebble thrown into the river, his memory will ripple across the ocean, yet
never touching all the lives he would have altered.
All his mother's dreams for him will disappear.

Look up in the dark night and see
one bright new star to shine
for Adam
who died
today.

About the Author

Leilani Ruland was born in Hawaii and raised in Ohio. She trained at Camden Clark Memorial Hospital in Parkersburg, West Virginia. She studied writing at The Ohio State University. She has lived in both Germany and Poland. She now resides with her husband and two cats in Marietta, Ohio.

She is the author of three books:

Baby Lost: From the Diary of a Neonatal Nurse

In My Father's Poland

Cadillac Ambulances – The Wild Ride of a Diploma Nurse in Training